Maa & Pa, I Love You

A Collection of Poems Dedicated to
Mothers
& Fathers

Charu Bhatnagar

BookLeaf
Publishing

India | USA | UK

Copyright © Charu Bhatnagar
All Rights Reserved.

This book has been self-published with all reasonable efforts taken to make the material error-free by the author. No part of this book shall be used, reproduced in any manner whatsoever without written permission from the author, except in the case of brief quotations embodied in critical articles and reviews.

The Author of this book is solely responsible and liable for its content including but not limited to the views, representations, descriptions, statements, information, opinions, and references ["Content"]. The Content of this book shall not constitute or be construed or deemed to reflect the opinion or expression of the Publisher or Editor. Neither the Publisher nor Editor endorse or approve the Content of this book or guarantee the reliability, accuracy, or completeness of the Content published herein and do not make any representations or warranties of any kind, express or implied, including but not limited to the implied warranties of merchantability, fitness for a particular purpose.

The Publisher and Editor shall not be liable whatsoever...

Made with ❤ on the BookLeaf Publishing Platform

www.bookleafpub.in
www.bookleafpub.com

Dedication

Dedicated to my mother and

father. Thank You, Mummy and

Papa, for dreaming with me, and for

me.

Acknowledgement

First and foremost, I would like to express my deepest gratitude to BookLeaf Publishing for providing me with this wonderful opportunity to publish my poetry book. This is a privilege I will cherish forever, as this book would not have come to life without the opportunity you granted me.

I would also like to extend my heartfelt thanks to my parents, whose unwavering encouragement and belief in my dreams have been my greatest strength. Without their support, I might have given up on striving to better myself.

Thank you, Mummy and Papa, for always being there for me. To my extended family—my brother, Bhabhi, niece, and sister—thank you all for seeing the best in me and my poetry.

—Charu Bhatnagar

Preface

The first book for any writer or poet holds a special place—it is a dream come true, and a milestone to be cherished. Like any other writer, I too wanted to savor this dream to the fullest and make it as meaningful as possible.

With this in mind, I decided to dedicate this once-in-a-lifetime opportunity to my parents, Who have always encouraged me to take my passion for storytelling and poetry seriously and to hone my skills. Their unwavering support inspired the central theme of this poetry book: *Mother and Father.*

Out of the twenty-one poems in this collection, ten are dedicated to *Mother,* ten to Father and one to both. Through these poems, I have attempted to highlight the unique qualities of mothers and fathers and capture memories that many children might relate to. I have enjoyed highlighting the qualities of mothers and fathers; highlighting the love for them.

I hope that as much as I have rejoiced in writing these poems, the readers will find something within these pages that touches your hearts as well.

—Charu Bhatnagar

1. You Are The Universe

The blue of your sky fills me with hope,
freedom, optimism, and shelter.
To be as free as a bird, rule like an eagle, and
aim like a
Falcon— the formidable hunter.
Your sunshine guides me during the long,
warm, and
sometimes too hot days of life.
Your moonlight and starshine enlightening
my pathway
Through the dark and difficult nights.

I stumble my way through, yet you always
ground me,

as good as the Earth might,
The nourishment of your love, like a farmer's
crop,
Gifts of the fruits of your labour is a sight.
I continue to strive and move along your
ever-flowing rivers, absorbing the lessons they
carry.
Finding further wisdom and strength from
your tall
mountains, lest I perish and forget to parry.

Learning the depths and unpredictability of
life from your vast and varied oceans,
Knowing that I am safe as long as I am near
the volcano
You can be for my protection.
You are all these entities and much more,
Mother,
And I am proud to be your child,
You are 'the universe' itself and I present to
you this ode,
From my emotions running too wild.

-Charu Bhatnagar

2. You Are A Teacher

Mother, you became a teacher the moment
you brought me to life,
My first lesson from you might as well have
been what it is to smile.
Do I wish to remember all those moments of
a tiny, vulnerable child?
But I do crave to be the same baby, grateful
for your light.

I stumbled, and you taught me to walk—a
lesson I had still sought,
Did you understand what I said, even when I
babytalked?
Even now, fumbling in my speeches, I seek
your motivational parts,
Throwing tantrums still, I inevitably forget
to learn from your heart.

I knew not how to navigate the world, and
you taught me that kindness was a start,
How to be alert, firm, disciplined, and
resilient in this world, which is hard.
You taught me to live my dreams, *Mother,*
and to dream big deeds and goals,
Mother, you are 'a teacher', my first
guru—sings to you
my thankful soul.

-Charu Bhatnagar

3. You Are Patience

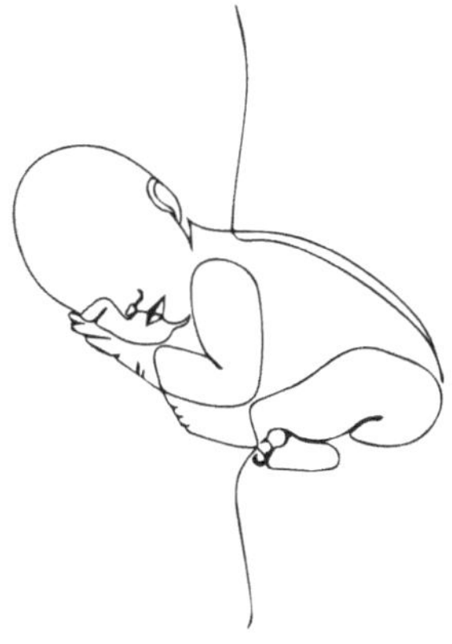

The tears and helplessness of a confused
infant,
For your loving arms, they were no deterrent.
Loud wails invading the peace of the night,
Yet you bore the noise, calling me your light.

Might have I been a toddler with loud
outbursts?
But your maternal voice never uttered a curse.
Tears of separation when I first went to
school,
Did your eyes water, or did you keep your
cool?

From school complaints to teenage rebellions,
All my troubles to you were worth a million.
Through adult complexities and a depressed
countenance,
You are 'patience', *Mother*, to persevere with
my consequences.

-Charu Bhatnagar

4. You Are Anger

The child laughed, cried, and found new
words to use,
Your motherly anger was a disparate emotion
with the Terrible Twos.
Mischief of a toddler, innocence and laughter
of childhood,
Always ending in some naughtiness for you
to rebuke.

Teachers' complaints of failures and
incompetence,
Your scolding was still the instrument that
fueled my confidence.

If the child forgot your moral lessons, you let
your temper loose,
You, *Mother*, are 'the rightful anger' my
success will always choose.

-Charu Bhatnagar

5. You Are Forgiveness

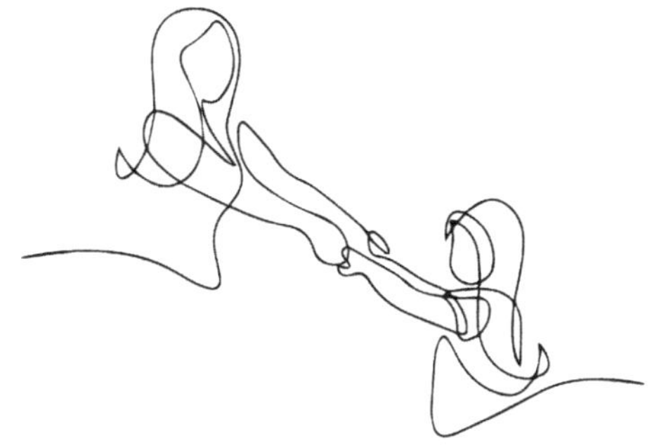

You corrected my alphabets until I got them
right as I cried,
And celebrated my mastery of lessons with
joy and pride.
Forbidding me sometimes from joining
school trips,
I fuelled my resentment while meals for me-
you continued to whip.

Blaming you for every misplaced, ruined, or
lost thing of mine,
You continued to lend your shoulder to me
when I needed to cry.
I loitered time on friends, laughter and
sharing food with them,

While you invariably waited for me each time
with nothing to gain.

I lose in life and find myself trapped in the
hell of depression,
You become my comfort, enduring my
misplaced irritation.
Continuing to wake before me, you still give
me everything,
You, *Mother*, are 'forgiveness', the sunshine I
am always seeking.

-Charu Bhatnagar

6. You Are Sacrifice

Giving up your comforts long before the
children are born,
You neglect your health, even when we show
scorn.
Every day you fight with yourself and time
just for our sakes,
We pray to be as caring and duty-bound
when it's our turn to repay.

I remember spewing my guts out late at night
in terrible stomach pain,
You stayed awake to calm me, running to the
doctor through heavy rain.

I burn the midnight oil, and whole day
last-minute studying prevails,
While you exhaust yourself alone in the
kitchen, keeping me fed still lest I fail.

Life turns into a disaster frequently, I panic
and toil, still feeling like a failure,
A disaster turns into depression while you
continue to be my savior.
My eyes open in this world and you give me
your sunshine,
My eyes close and you become my own
starlight,
You, *Mother,* are 'sacrifice' burning away your
oil for lighting up our thankless lives;
consistently paying the price.

-Charu Bhatnagar

7. You Are 'Mother Nurture'

The first morning, the new excitement, the
first fear, and the first school day of my life,
I received my first lesson from you: to be a
dedicated student and not adopt a bullying
style.
My tears and woes find your embrace as the
days of
being a bullied child, to you I narrate,
You counsel me, saying this is nothing but a
stepping stone, and there
are more fountains of success to satiate.

I find your love in the green of grass,the
fragrance of flowers, and the colours of birds,
Walking with my feet on the lap of nature is
one of the divine habits
you taught me should be treasured.
The feel of paper and the smell of books is
among
the first gifts from you I remember and still
have addiction,
From finding inspiration in tales of heroes
unforgettable to finding awe and romance in
the visuals of fiction.

From my failed music classes to failing to
internalize other important talents,
You encourage me through all my eventual
laziness to present my best front.
I stumble through the pathways life offers
and get lost in the many possible goals,
You are my *'Mother Nurture',* who taught me
the best ways in life to roll.
-Charu Bhatnagar

8. You Are Ocean

I am a droplet of your expansive ocean with
its great depths,
Apart from the seas but still a deep part of
the water chests.
I flow where your ocean waves trend, go
where your wishes are complimentary,
Never do I forget to fight occasionally to
assert my righteous self-identity.

Dropping and falling repeatedly to the depths
where your seabed lies,
Then to be guided by your gentleness to the
top where your surface attempts to touch the
skies.
High winds of the world drive me into
storming and devastating tides,

You pull me back to your brine, giving me a
new normal life.

Influenced by the Moon and Sun, we are
evermore pulled and pushed,
Divine gravity notwithstanding, your
strength nevermore will I overlook.
Under your shelter, I grow and grow until I,
too, attempt to become a refuge,
You, *Mother,* are 'ocean', to whom your
droplets will always owe- a debt huge.
-Charu Bhatnagar

9. You Are Encouragement

Remembrance of my childhood before school
and realizations of an imperfect vision,
You became my light, my eyes, and the
guiding hands with the warmth of the Sun.
Memories of constant tears, bullied moments
when a-friendless me is left heartbroken,
You become my healing balm, to pick up
those shattered pieces lest they become
frozen.

Disappointments of a new school, new
bullies, and the still misunderstood child I
used to be,
Academic merits in school to faltering marks,
and
losing the social learning degree.
You become the haven for my sobbing heart,
For home was wherever you were even apart.
Learning to be unhappy since a young age,
Only your presence could break my own cage.

Lamentations of my present, when I still need
your words of love to continue on life's path,
Innumerable collections of moments when
you had to uplift me, for me to just restart.
Depression becomes my constant companion;
only your tutelage heartening me to not fall
in dark,
You, my *Mother*, are 'encouragement', even
when I underestimate you and ridicule you to
generally be a nark.
-Charu Bhatnagar

10. You Are Strength

The mountain across the gorge looks
enticing, full of mysteries, rewards, and
beauty,
My own on this side seems too mundane, too
used to, bound by mere duty.
You pull me back, returning the focus of my
distracted gaze on the greens of our own hill,
That, admirable might be the visuals of
sunrise on the other hill but,
 there is beauty even in our own chills.

Sometimes when the chill feels too long and
strong, if the forced liveliness is even worth it
I wonder,

Ready for a break and to celebrate some
sunshine, to the
other hill I am about to wander.
In search of a new, definitive path I never
found, I am
ready to embark knowing it's not an
adventure.
You show me the abundance of beautiful yet
difficult
paths here, helping my mind to center.

The thirst in my throat shows the
never-ending dissatisfaction with our hills
and our own springs,
To explore the probable sweetness in the
fountains of the other hill my eyes don't stop
to blink,
Maybe my unfulfilled cravings will be sated in
a place where so far I had always been a
failure,
But you, *Mother,* are 'the strength' of nature,
guiding me uninhibited, the ways to show-
winning valor.
-Charu Bhatnagar

11. You Are Security

Lone wails and endless tears of that little
infant child pierce the air,
Your arms form a cocoon, protecting the
child from every despair.
Helpless, powerless head and flailing arms
plead for some warmth,
Your hand on their head and the other
around remain the most comforting forms.

The innocence of that new kid first time
embarking to any school,
The child never recognized the shields of your
love there, warm like wool.

Confusing concepts, unyielding subjects, and
mistakes in tests,
Your voice and presence, like a Phoenix, and
the child won't ever be stressed.

The unending experiences of that
now-grown-up child,
in a chilled-up cruel world,
Sometimes, all that a child needs still is your
hand on head,
to let the grievances unfold.
To let you see the fire of determination, and
light of success in the error-filled eyes,
You, *Father*, are 'the security' of every child,
the need continuing even in their adult life.
-Charu Bhatnagar

12. You Are Sky

Tiny new sapling underneath the infinitely
expansive welkin,
Assured of adequate warmth and water,
wherever it's dwelling;
Fear of being damaged or destroyed by your
sometimes volatile skies,
But the sapling always looks up to your
strength and magnanimity, even without
eyes.

The sapling grows up, watching stars and the
moon adorning the sky's lapel,

Aiming to please the sky, the sapling secretly
desires to grow just as high, and excel.
An insurmountable task it is, the sapling
realizes to even touch the greatness of the
ether,
To best realize its own potential is the only
option the sapling decides, as it were.

Sometimes surrounded by stones, sometimes
by soft soil, the sapling is always afraid.
"Am I alone?" the sapling wonders, but your
vast sure presence proves that you cared.
Unappreciated and underestimated, the
company, the celestial blue of the sky gives,
You, *Father*, are 'the sky' with your protective
and providing envelope.
-Charu Bhatnagar

13. Knightly Father

She was the little princess of the house, her
father a king like knight,
He protected her from the dark and cuddled
her through every fright.
When the clouds influenced her judgment, he
shone his own guiding light,
He was her favourite hero, whose actions
were just and his justice, always right.

Stories famous, some untold, the knight read
and told to the princess every night,

Her father's voice and his loving arms around
her was the princess's favourite night-time
sight.
Dreading the mornings and the loss to school
time, daily tormenting fights,
She looked forward to the evenings when her
knightly father played Badminton with her
outside.

Time grew, with it grew the princess and
grew did her own opinions wild,
"I know everything, sometimes more than
you. I'm not a child no more," she cried.
Told the princess to her still worried knight
like *Father* in a temper all riled,
Yet you my 'Knightly Father', are my
forevermore shield, my love for you all piled.
-Charu Bhatnagar

14. His Hands

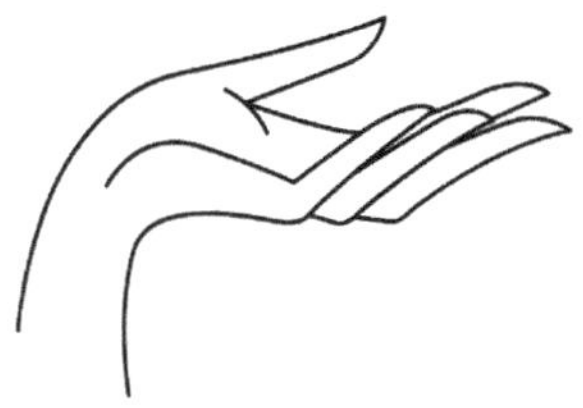

The tiny tot in his arms, his hand there was to
support their head,
To envelope the child in his protection, and
carry them to the play set.
Strong and playful hands, steady enough to
allow the bairn on it to stand,
Your hands were a vision of joy and security,
unplanned.

His hands dealt out the punishments if
justified beforehand,
Bad marks or misdemeanours, yet your love
always transcends.
Guiding and teaching hands, leading his
"little child" to just lands,
Your hands, a constant educator, even
through lessons lost like sand.

The child, an adult and grown up not too
naïve still sought his hands,
A welcoming pat on the back and a warm
touch of reassurance on head,
His encouraging smile goes a long way to
make the heart of child say thanks,
You, *Father*, are that perfect father for whose
wellbeing I can only chant.
-Charu Bhatnagar

15. My Forever Idol

Though I never watched you, Daddy, leaving
home to make your parents proud,
To set and achieve new milestones of success
and to struggle without a shout.
Turning your smallest achievements into
your biggest triumphs,
You, I heard, were infallibly positive and
different, never quite a part of the crowd.

Most selfless and dutiful, indulged in the
familial and official service,
I often wish to inculcate at the least a small
percent of your sense of justice.
Every day you set for yourself new standards
which are essentially hard to dismiss,

Dismayed I am though for not inheriting
your brilliance and inspiring gifts.

I see you now, retired, elderly certainly not
ready to break your willpower,
Eager and ready to learn new skills even if it is
a lousy unfocused teacher.
To make the best of your time you strive and
consistently make the time right,
You, my *Father*, are my 'forever idol' who
never does anything out of spite.
-Charu Bhatnagar

16. Bed-time Stories

Remembering the earliest memories of you,
Papa, telling me daily bed-time stories,
Of you telling me answers before I ever
indulged in bombarding you with queries.
Those stories became sleep-time dreams,
invigorating me to create my own fantasies.

Fables of becoming your own hero, of loving
yourself and nature's buddies,
Of how ordinary men and women become
legends; their short biographies,
Inspiring the bullied child in me to overcome
my inhibitions and envisioning
some trophies.

I have lost much now, and much of myself,
always ashamed
to not reach your, desired victories,
Yet I still reach though for your words, for
encouragement and be better than my
histories,
Will you again tell me a story, Papa, so I can
hope for some better future trajectories?
-Charu Bhatnagar

17. Playing Badminton

For years in evenings, you, *Father,* played
with me,
with badminton rackets and shuttle of good
opportunities,
Vitalizing and joyous thoughts to look
forward to everyday, to our own time for our
family,
Teaching sports for fun and for the hope that
some values stick to me
  without becoming casualties.

Now here I am, never learning how to not
waste good opportunities;
nor is there any Badminton in the evenings,
Losing the chances life threw my way, but I
did learn how not to do any cheating,
Will you teach me again, *Father*, the game of
Opportunities?
For you it is, that I want my successes to keep
repeating.
-Charu Bhatnagar

18. Life Grade Card

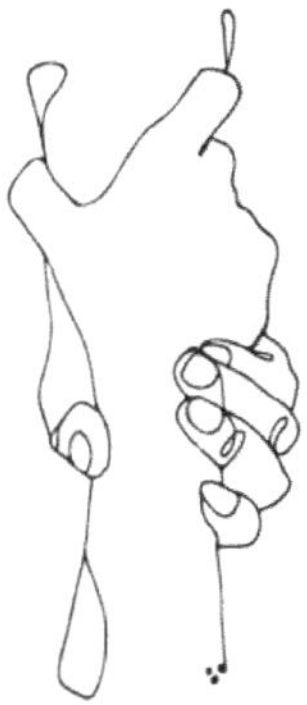

The school was small, and the report card
quite average,
Your hopeful presence still gave my heart
quiet courage.
A ruined, fearful day made marvelous with
what you salvaged,
I always yearned to do something to see your
pride-filled visage.

Now the life school is vast, but my report
card is well below average,
You still try to give me courage despite my
unappreciative language,

My yearning rusted, knowing the record of
my life tests reportage,
You wait still for my report card, maybe
hoping once more
that I will be a meritorious candidate.

Schoolmates with riches, reports, and records
of careers exemplary,
My eyes search for you now, even if I am
scoring lowest
and it is only temporary.
Losing my will but not my courage when
your presence is a reminder of possibilities,
Will you, *Father*, still check my 'Life Grade
Card' and teach me how to handle
responsibilities?
-Charu Bhatnagar

19. Are You That Juniper?

The one that protects the house from evil and its classifications universal, are you that Juniper?
The Father protecting his home, with his variations global and the inhabitants of home his centre,
To survive climates of life extreme for the duty of life,
harsh conditions- the Juniper and you, weather.

The one that grows slow, steady but surely
into strength,
wisdom, and beauty of soul,
are you that Juniper?
You, who is known to shine the brightest in
the trickiest and riskiest situations,
be it drought or thunder,
Self-pruning and shedding, like a Juniper
you do,
your self-discipline is a wonder.

The one that nurtures and cures-its berries
are a meal for humans and birds alike,
are you that Juniper?
For centuries the child was nurtured and
healed by a Father,
the hunger sated by his fruits of labour.
Acts like a counter-poison and purification,
yes, Juniper does.
Like so you are my energy to counter
negativity and confusion
since you are my pater.
-Charu Bhatnagar

20. The Sun, The Cloud

&

The Moon

Rising early in routine, and you are off to the
duties of home and work,
Without any leave for your own, only for the
family do you use your perks.
Providing warmth in the winter and light and
energy in many ways,
You, *Father*, are the sun during the short and
long sunny days.

Bestowing us with shadows during
unbearable, unhealthy day heat,
Awarding us with comfortable warmth that
helps to have the cold nights cheat.
Satiate our lives and nourish us wholly, even
if you are angry,
You, *Father*, are the cloud, indispensable for
the growth of our nursery.

Your gravity keeps us from falling off our
pathway axis,
Pulling our life's tides enough to impart us
with further purpose.
Shining and guiding with your soothing light
during dark,
You, *Father*, are the moon during the nights,
making your own mark.
- Charu Bhatnagar

21. Thank You Mum & Pa

Maybe I was too young to discern when you
had me and took care of my needs,
When you taught me to talk, walk and how
to self-feed,
Educated me in school and edified my life,
your person not superseded,
I could not thank you then Mum & Pa,
having not grown out of fluffy cheeks.

Maybe I was too concerned as a silent student
when you taught me everything you could,
Mathematics, English and tuitions in topics
which I would not hope to find and include.

Talking with my teachers even as I fought
with my words and win over my ineptitude,
I could not thank you then Mum & Pa,
though now aware of the sacrifices and
sometimes blues.

Maybe I was too depressed as a grown-up
adult since years past and now,
When you put up with my moods, but to
find my own path you always allowed,
Encouraging me even when I fail, for soon
you declared I may have reasons to say 'wow'.
Hence, this is me thanking you Mum & Pa
for every blessing on me you bestowed.
-Charu Bhatnagar